DATE DUE			APR 04
GAYLORD			PRINTED IN U.S.A.

Horses

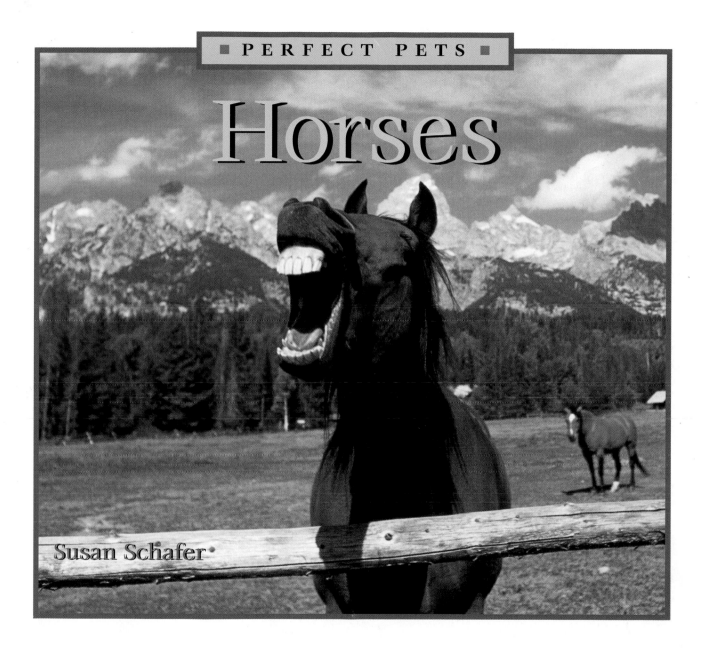

Susan Schafer

BENCHMARK BOOKS

MARSHALL CAVENDISH

Benchmark Books
Marshall Cavendish
99 White Plains Road
Tarrytown, New York 10591

Library of Congress Cataloging-in-Publication Data

Schafer, Susan.
Horses/by Susan Schafer.
p.cm. – (Perfect pets)
Includes bibliographical references and index.
Summary: Presents information on various breeds of horses, including their evolution and history, physical characteristics, behavior, and the basics of caring for horse.
ISBN 0-7614-1395-2
1. Horses—Juvenile literature. [1.Horses.] I. Title. II. Series.

SF302.S32 2002
636.1—dc21

2001043800

Photo Research by Candlepants Incorporated

Cover Photo: Animals Animals/ Robert Maier

The photographs in this book are used by permission and through the courtesy of: Photo Researchers, Inc.: Porterfield-Chickering, 1; Tom McHugh, 10; E.R. Degginger, 14; Elisabeth Weiland, 19 (right), 23; Jim Grace. 22 (left); Margaret Miller, 25 (right); Bonnie Rauch, 26, 28; Laima Druskis, 27. Animals Animals: Carol Geake, 3; Henry Ausloos, 9; Eastcott/MomatuiK, 12; Robert Maier, 13, 14(left), 15, 19(left), 22(right), back cover; Ralph Reinhold, 16; Bob Langrish, 18; Susan Ley, 20; Barbara Reed, 24; Tom Edwards, 25(left). Dept. of Library Services, American Museum of Natural History, photo #313408 by H.S. Rice: 4. Art Resource, NY: British Museum London, photo by Eric Lessing, 6; Giradon, 7; Nimatallah, 8.

Printed in Hong Kong
6 5 4 3 2 1

Thanks to Cheyenne Love, Brooke Love, Paul Severtson, and Richard Gearhart for reviewing this manuscript, and to Dr. Brad Hollstein, D.V.M., for taking his time to answer my questions. A special thanks to Connye Oker for her time and consideration in contributing ideas for this book.

The prehistoric horse Mesohippus had three toes.

Swishing

its tail at a fly, a horse munches on leaves. Suddenly, its head comes up. Its ears turn forward to listen. A branch rustles in the distance. The horse turns and runs, its hooves pounding the ground. Ducking into the brush, it hides in the forest.

You are in North America fifty million years ago. The horse stands a foot high at the shoulders. If it was standing next to you, its back would barely reach your knees. It is the first horse—the dawn horse— but it looks more like a small dog with a tail like a donkey's. It has four toes on its front feet. Each toe has a tiny hoof.

The dawn horse existed until the weather in North America changed millions of years later. The forests disappeared. Grasslands replaced the forests. There were fewer places for the horses to hide. Only those that ran the fastest could escape from predators.

Stone carvings at least two thousand years old show horses pulling chariots into battle.

The faster horses were born with only three toes on each foot. They survived, so when their young were born, they also had three toes. Over time, more and more horses had three toes. Slowly, the dawn horse was replaced by the three-toed horse.

Millions more years passed. Eventually, the first one-toed horse appeared. It had only its middle toe, so it could turn and run even faster.

Then, during the **Ice Age**, about two million years ago, the sea level fell several hundred feet. A strip of land was uncovered between what are now Alaska and Russia. The **descendants** of the first one-toed horse left North America across this strip of land, moving into Asia and the rest of the **Old World**. They spread out to eventually evolve into zebras, donkeys, and more horses. The tundra horse lived far in the north, in what is now Siberia. It had thick fur to fight the cold. The forest horse, with large hooves for walking in swamps, lived in the wet forests of Europe. The tarpan, slender and swift, lived in the dry regions of eastern Europe and western Russia.

The sons of noblemen and kings, like young Alexander the Great, learned to ride early.

Traces of Toes

Bucephalus was the horse ridden by Alexander the Great, who ruled a large kingdom covering Greece, Egypt, and western Asia about two thousand years ago. Stories and drawings of Bucephalus show that it had three toes just like its ancient **ancestors**. Horses today are rarely born with three toes, but they do have "chestnuts" on the insides of their knees and **hocks**. Chestnuts look like thick calluses. They are the traces of hooves that were once connected to toes. Very rarely, a horse is born with extra toes just like its ancient ancestors.

A medieval knight and his horse are ready to ride into battle.

As the horses migrated to Europe, they disappeared from North America. They might never have returned if not for the Spanish explorers who brought them back in the sixteenth century. By then, people had been taming horses in the Old World for about five thousand years.

At first, horses were used for meat and milk. Later, they pulled chariots and plows. They carried soldiers and supplies. As they became more useful, people began **breeding** them for special features. For example, by mating their largest horses, they got larger young. In this way, people in different places created new **breeds** of horses. Then they bred the new horses together to make even more breeds. Now, there are more than three hundred different kinds!

Each breed is described in a special book, or **registry**. To be registered, a horse must have the right ancestors, body shape, size, **gait**, and sometimes color, for that breed. Not all horses are registered, however. Many people have wonderful horses that are mixes of different breeds.

The palomino—with a coat the color of a shiny coin—is a popular horse.

A Horse of a Different Color

A horse can be many different colors. Gray, chestnut, palomino, and bay are a few different-colored breeds. White horses are really called grays, unless they are albinos. Grays have dark eyes, black skin, and white and black hairs. They are born dark and slowly turn white with age. Albinos are born with pink skin, all-white hair, and blue or red eyes. Chestnuts are usually red-gold, but can be as dark as chocolate. Palominos have gold hair with a white mane and tail. Bays are brown with black legs, mane, and tail. Although the colors are beautiful, the wise horseperson never chooses a horse by color alone. It's a horse's personality that counts.

Strong and low to the ground, small ponies were first bred to pull carts of coal or peat.

A horse

is a horse, of course, but what is a pony? It is a horse, one that is usually small when it is grown. Horse breeds are grouped into ponies, light horses, and heavy horses. Ponies have stocky bodies, short legs, and thick fur. They are descendants of the early horses from the north. The Shetland pony, for example, came from the tundra horse.

Most ponies stand nine to fourteen and a half hands high. That is the measurement from the ground to the top of the horse's **withers**, or shoulders. Long ago, people used their hands to measure a horse. Now, one hand is equal to four inches (ten centimeters).

Most horses are light horses. They are usually taller than ponies, around fifteen to seventeen hands. With longer bodies and slimmer legs, they are built for riding. The Arabian, Thoroughbred, quarter horse, paint, and Appaloosa are just a few.

When given a choice, horses will always choose to be close to other horses.

The Arabian is a very old breed. Some believe it is descended from the tarpan. It was used to breed other light horses, such as the Thoroughbred. The Thoroughbred is the fastest horse, racing at up to thirty-five miles per hour. The next time you ride in a car, ask the driver how fast that is.

One, Two, Three, Gallop!

A **gait** is a special way of walking or running. Horses have four basic gaits—walk, trot, canter, and gallop. The walk is a four-beat gait. Each hoof hits the ground at a different time. If you listen when you ride, you can hear each hoof hit: one, two, three, four...one, two, three, four.... Speed the horse up a little and he trots. The trot is a two-beat gait: one, two...one, two.... Two hooves hit the ground together. First, the front right and the back left. Then the front left and the back right. Speed up a little more and the horse canters. The canter is a three-beat gait: one, two, three...one, two, three.... One hoof hits, then two together, and then one. The fastest gait is the gallop. It has four beats and a moment when the horse is suspended in the air, with all four feet up off the ground!

The Appaloosa gets its name from the Palouse River valley, where the Nez Percé Indians once lived.

Percheron stallions, like this one, are often use to pull wagons and coaches.

Mustangs are descended from the Spanish horses that the Europeans brought to North America. Native Americans, settlers, and cowboys caught them for riding, carrying loads, and pulling plows.

Appaloosas and paints were bred from mustangs to have blotched or spotted coats. The paint looks as if it has been splashed with large blotches of paint. The Appaloosa, bred by the Nez Percé Indians, is spotted. The spots are usually shades of red.

Heavy horses are also called draft horses. They are descendants of the forest horse. Although they are heavy and strong, they are not always tall. Some are as short as a quarter horse. Most stand between sixteen and seventeen hands. They have carried knights in armor and pulled wagons and plows.

The largest drafts, such as the shire and Percheron, are often over seventeen hands. Imagine trying to climb onto a refrigerator. That's how high their backs are. The largest horse ever was a Percheron which stood twenty-one hands and weighed over three thousand

When a horse feels good, it runs and kicks up his heels.

pounds. If you and your friends weighed sixty pounds each, it would take more than fifty of you to weigh this much.

Which horse breed is the best? There isn't one. Horses have many uses, so each person must find the right horse for him or her.

Some horses are working horses. They are used on farms and ranches, and in rodeos. They are ridden by mounted police and raced by jockeys. Many horses are kept as pets for trail riding, jumping, or carriage driving. Horses are not typical pets, however. They are big and expensive and need special care. If you want to own a horse, you will have to understand these needs.

Two young Thoroughbreds say hello.

A horse

can't speak, but it can let you know how its feeling. When it is happy, it prances with its tail in the air. When it is angry, it pins down its ears. When it is afraid, it snorts or runs away. Pet horses must be trained not to run away from things they fear.

Training should be done only by an experienced horse trainer. Horses naturally kick and bite each other. They buck up in the air. But it would be dangerous to let them do those things around people. They must learn to control their natural habits so people can work around them and ride them safely. Veterinarians and horse clubs in your area can recommend good horse trainers.

Horses say hello to each other by touching noses. They recognize each other's smells. Because they live in herds, they like company. They choose special friends to stay close to. If you keep a horse alone, you will be his only friend and will need to spend lots of time with him.

With its long neck and tail raised, an Arabian shows its spirit.

In a herd, one horse is the "top horse"—the boss of all the others. Another is second. It bosses every horse except the top horse. A third bosses everyone but the first two, and so on down the line. Horses that get picked on too much by others in their herd may not eat well. They need to be fed separately.

When you own a horse, you become part of its herd. If it bites or kicks you, it is trying to be the boss. It needs immediate training by an expert horseperson. Horses should learn that people are always the "top horses."

In the wild, a male horse is called a **stallion**. One stallion in the herd is always the top horse. It protects the herd, so it has to be strong and aggressive. Stallions bite and kick each other to establish which is the top horse. Because they are aggressive, they are usually not safe to keep as pets. People who do keep stallions must keep them away from each other in pens. Geldings are stallions that have been "fixed," or neutered, so they can no longer produce babies. They make gentler pets and can be kept with other horses.

18

Playing helps foals develop strong muscles.

Horses use their sharp eyes and ears to sense danger.

Female horses are called **mares**. Baby horses are called **foals**. **Fillies** are female foals under four years old, and **colts** are male foals, also under four years old. Horses become adults at two years but aren't fully grown until they are five. They can live for thirty years or more.

A horse's eyes are on the sides of his head. It can see in almost every direction without moving. However, it has blind spots just in front of its nose and right behind its ear. For that reason, never walk up behind a horse. If you startle it, it might kick you. Approach it from the side and talk to it so it knows you're there.

A horse has sensitive ears. Its ears usually point where it is looking, but it can turn one ear forward and the other back to listen in two directions. It is also sensitive to touch. It can feel a fly land on its skin as easily as you can.

When you ride a horse, you need only the slightest touch to tell a horse what to do. If you touch its sides with your heels and it doesn't trot, you don't need to kick it harder. It felt you the first time. It is just ignoring you. What it really needs is more training to teach it to move when you ask it to.

A brush and comb are a must for keeping a horse clean and tidy.

Taking

care of a horse is hard work. You must check, feed, water, groom, and clean up after it every day—no matter what.

Caring for a horse takes patience. Losing your temper or beating a horse only makes it more frightened or nervous. If it isn't behaving, it needs training, not anger.

Owning and caring for a horse is expensive. You'll need lessons to learn how to ride one safely. You'll have to buy boots and a helmet. Your horse will need food, water, **tack**, such as a saddle and bridle, and a **farrier** to trim its hooves or put on horseshoes. It needs a veterinarian for checkups, vaccinations, medicine, and care if it gets sick. It also needs ample room for exercise and a stable.

Gee, Where's the Knee?

A horse has the same body parts as you. They're just in different places. Its elbows are at the top of its front legs, close to its body. Its knees are really like your wrists. The true knees of a horse, called **stifles**, are at the top of the back legs. Hocks are actually ankles and heels. They are higher than your ankles because horses stand on their toes. If you stand on tip-toe, you'll see your heels sticking out in back like a horse's hocks.

Take care where you ride your horse. Hard or rough ground can hurt a horse's legs.

A mare licks and nuzzles her foal.

Read as many horse books as you can. Learn about the horse's body, health, and care. Talk to your veterinarian, trainer, and other horse people. The more information you get, the better decisions you and your family will make.

Before you get a horse, know what kind of rider you are, what kind of horse you want, and what you will use it for. Are you an experienced rider or a beginner? Do you want a quiet quarter horse for trail riding, or a lively Arabian for cross-country racing? Your horse should match your abilities.

Unless you know how to train a horse yourself or are able to get an experienced trainer, you should consider getting an older, well-trained horse. Horses are taken from their mothers at about six months—this is called **weaning**—but they cannot be ridden until they are about two years old. Before that, they are still growing.

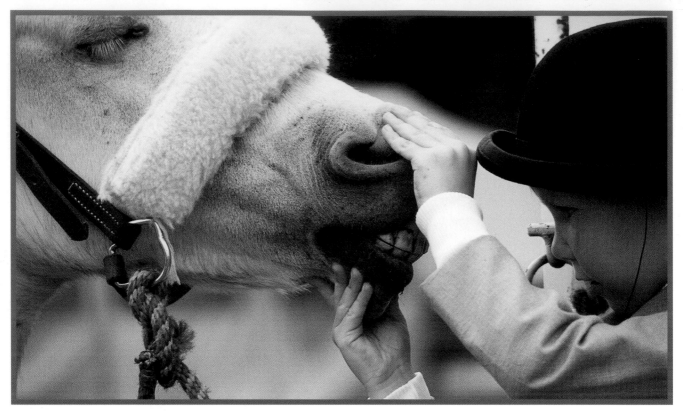

A foal's baby teeth (milk teeth) are replaced by permanent teeth by the age of five.

Show Me Those Pearly Whites

Horses have cutting teeth at the front of their mouths. They use the cutting teeth to chop off grass as they graze. At the backs of their mouths, they have grinding teeth that grind up the grass. In between the cutting teeth and the grinding teeth is a space that has no teeth at all. When you put a bridle on a horse, the bit goes in the mouth and fits into that space. Mares have thirty-six teeth, but stallions and geldings have forty. The extra four teeth are called bridle teeth because they grow in the space where the bridle bit goes. If the bridle teeth get in the way of the bit, they are removed.

Feeding a horse by hand can sometimes encourage it to nip or bite.

A manure fork is used to "muck out" pens.

Ask your veterinarian, farrier, or an experienced horseperson to recommend a reputable horse breeder or horse farm. Then shop with an adult who knows horses. If you find the right horse, whether it's a young horse or older, go back several times before you buy. Walk up to it and pet it on the neck to see how it acts, but only if you're sure it's safe. It should stand calmly. See if you can brush it and if it lets you pick up Its legs. If it is in a pen, it should come to you willingly, not run away. Can you lead it and ride it? If not, then this may not be the right horse for you.

Finally, have a veterinarian check it. This may cost a little more, but it's worth it. You don't want to find out something is wrong with your horse after you get it home.

At home, have a shelter with at least three sides to protect your horse from the weather. Horses don't need heated shelters, but they do need to be protected from drafts and cold winds. Each side of the shelter should be at least twelve feet (four meters) long and eight feet (two meters) high. Four-sided shelters need a large door with a window. Horses like to see what's going on around them. The floor needs a thick layer of wood shavings or straw to keep it from getting muddy and smelly.

Don't feed a horse on dirt or sand—swallowing it can make it sick.

The shelter should open to a fenced pen or pasture. The larger, the better. Horses in small pens get bored. They pick up bad habits like chewing wood, which can wear down teeth, and gulping air, which can cause **colic**. Check the pen every day. Remove poisonous plants, broken glass, metal, wire, or anything that might hurt your horse.

There is no simple recipe for feeding your horse. It depends on where you live, what is available, what kind of horse you have, and how much exercise it gets. A mixture of alfalfa and grass hay is excellent. Very active horses may need supplements, such as pellets or grain. Ask your veterinarian what he or she recommends. Sudden food changes can make horses colic.

Colic is a stomach illness that causes pain, and even death. A horse with colic stops eating. It will look or kick at its belly with its back feet. It might lie down, groan, or roll over again and again. If this happens, call your veterinarian immediately. Overeating can also cause colic, so keep extra food locked up.

A police horse must always be calm, even in the heavy traffic and noise of a city.

Whatever you feed your horse, it should be clean, fresh, sweet, and dry. Horses need to eat at least twice a day. Give your horse a mineral block, which is a large chunk of salt mixed with vitamins and minerals, such as calcium. Your horse will lick it whenever he needs to.

Horses can drink twelve gallons of water every day. That's the same as forty-eight liter bottles of soda pop! Keep a **trough** full of fresh, cool (not ice-cold) water. Check it every day to see how much your horse drinks. A sick horse may stop drinking.

Brush your horse and clean its feet with a hoof pick daily. As you work, check for injuries like cuts and rashes. Report any problems to a veterinarian right away.

Ask ten different people why they like horses and you'll probably get ten different answers. To a jockey, a horse means speed and glory, to a mounted police officer, a working partner. For a person not able to walk, a horse becomes its legs. If you had a horse, what would it mean to you?

Fun Facts

A horse can sleep standing up by locking the joints in its legs.

You can tell how old a horse is by how much its teeth have worn down.

A mule is a cross between a male donkey and a mare. A hinny is a cross between a female donkey and a stallion.

The heaviest horse was a Belgian stallion that weighed 3,200 pounds (1,500 kilograms). Its hooves were 14 inches (36 centimeters) across, about as wide as a large pizza!

Settlers in early America bred a horse that could work their farms but also race on a course a quarter of a mile long. That's how the quarter horse got its name.

The smallest modern-day horse was a miniature horse that stood three and a half hands when it was two years old, in 1975. That is about as tall as a backpack!

Made of material like your fingernails, a horse's hooves grow an average of two and a half inches per year.

The strongest horse is the shire. A single shire once pulled thirty-two and a half tons, about the same weight as eight bull elephants!

In the earliest horse races, horses were not ridden. They were kept thirsty and turned loose to run to water.

Glossary

ancestor: an early kind of animal from which later kinds have developed.

breeding: keeping animals in pairs so they will have young.

breed: a special type of some animal or plant.

colic: a stomach illness that can cause pain or death in horses.

colt: a young male horse; a young stallion.

descendant: a living thing that came from a certain ancestor.

farrier: someone who shoes horses.

filly: a young female horse.

foal: a young horse, donkey, or similar animal.

gait: a way of walking or running.

hock: the joint in the middle of a horse's back leg that bends backward. It is similar to a human ankle.

Ice Age: a time, many years ago, when ice covered much of the earth.

mare: a female horse, donkey, or similar animal.

Old World: the Eastern Hemisphere—Europe, Asia, and Africa.

registry: a book that describes the characteristics of a breed of horse.

stallion: a male horse that can produce babies.

stifle: the joint in the middle of a horse's back leg that bends forward. It is similar to a human knee.

tack: a horse's equipment, such as saddle and bridle.

trough: a container that holds food or water for animals.

ungulate: any of a group of animals that has hooves, such as pigs, deer, and horses.

weaning: taking a young animal away from its mother.

withers: the highest part of a horse's back, between the shoulder blades.

Find Out More About Horses

Websites

Check out www.thehorse.com on the Web or the Nature Horse Page at
www.pbs.org/wnet/nature/horses

Ask questions and get answers about horses from a veterinarian at
groups.yahoo.com/groups/askavet

Books

Edwards, Elwyn Hartley. *Horses*. New York: Dorling Kindersley, 1993.

Hill, Cherry. *Stablekeeping: A Visual Guide to Safe and Healthy Horsekeeping*. Pownal, Vermont: Storey Books, 2000.

Jahiel, Jessica. *The Parent's Guide to Horseback Riding*. Los Angeles: Roxbury Park/Lowell House, 1999.

Vogel, Colin. *The Complete Horse Care Manual*. New York: Dorling Kindersley, 1995.

Index

About the Author

Susan Schafer has loved riding and working with horses for as long as she can remember. She now owns and trains her own horses on her ranch outside of San Luis Obispo, California, where she lives with her husband. She is a science teacher and the author of *Turtles*, *Lizards*, and *Snakes* in the Benchmark Books series Perfect Pets. In addition, she has written books about lions, tigers, vultures, the Galapagos tortoise, and the Komodo dragon.